Riches of the Earth

Sugar

Irene Franck and David Brownstone

GROLIER

An imprint of Scholastic Library Publishing
Danbury, Connecticut

Credits and Acknowledgments

abbreviations: t (top), b (bottom), l (left), r (right), c (center)
Image credits: Agricultural Research Service Library: 18r, 23, and 25r (Scott Bauer); CORBIS: 6 and 29 (James P. Blair), 27 (Archivo Iconografico, S.A.); Getty Images/PhotoDisc: 3 and 9l (Nancy R. Cohen), 5 (C Squared Studios), 10 (Ryan McVay), 11 (Mitch Hrdlicka), 12 (John A. Rizzo); Getty Images/PhotoDisc/PhotoLink: 4, 7, 8 (J. Luke), 19; National Aeronautics and Space Administration (NASA): 1t and running heads; National Geographic Society: 21 and 28 (James L. Stanfield); National Honey Board: 15; Photo Researchers, Inc.: 1b (Mark C. Burnett), 9r (Jan Robert Factor), 17 (John Mitchell), 18l (Scott Camazine), 20 (David Greenberg), 22l and 22r (A. B. Joyce), 25l (P. H. Leroux/Explorer), 26 (Nigel Cattlin/Holt Studios International); Photo Researchers, Inc./Science Photo Library: 13 (James King-Holmes), 14, 16 (Dr. Jeremy Burgess). Original image drawn for this book by K & P Publishing Services: 24.

Our thanks to Joe Hollander, Phil Friedman, and Laurie McCurley at Scholastic Library Publishing; to photo researchers Susan Hormuth, Robin Sand, and Robert Melcak; to copy editor Michael Burke; and to the librarians throughout the northeastern library network, in particular to the staff of the Chappaqua Library—director Mark Hasskarl; the expert reference staff, including Martha Alcott, Michele J. Capozzella, Maryanne Eaton, Catherine Paulsen, Jane Peyraud, Paula Peyraud, and Carolyn Reznick; and the circulation staff, headed by Barbara Le Sauvage—for fulfilling our wide-ranging research needs.

Published 2003 by Grolier
Division of Scholastic Library Publishing
Old Sherman Turnpike
Danbury, Connecticut 06816

For information address the publisher:
Scholastic Library Publishing, Grolier Division
Old Sherman Turnpike, Danbury, Connecticut 06816

Library of Congress Cataloging-in-Publication Data

Franck, Irene M.
    Sugar / Irene Franck and David Brownstone.
      p. cm. -- (Riches of the earth ; v. 13)
    Summary: Provides information about sugar and its importance in everyday life.
    Includes bibliographical references and index.
    ISBN 0-7172-5730-4 (set : alk. paper) -- ISBN 0-7172-5725-8 (vol. 13 : alk paper)
      1. Sugar--Juvenile literature [1. Sugar.] I. Brownstone, David M. II. Title.

TP378.2.F37 2003
664'.1--dc21

2003044092

Printed in the United States of America

Designed by K & P Publishing Services

Contents

Foods of all kinds, and most especially scrumptious desserts like the ones on this tray, are flavored with sugar.

Sugar Is Sweet

Sugar is sweet. Some of our favorite foods are sweetened with sugar, such as candy, ice cream, jellies, jams, cakes, cookies, and pies. Sugar is also found in other foods where we might not expect it. Some ketchups, for example, are 25 percent sugar! Sweetness is one of just a handful of tastes that are recognized by the taste buds on our tongues—though scientists do not know exactly why some foods taste sweet and others not.

Someone who really loves sugary foods is said to have a *sweet tooth*. In truth, our love of sugar has a sound basis. Sugar doesn't just taste good. It actually powers our bodies every second that we are alive.

There are many different kinds of sugars (see p. 7). However, the

No matter what kinds of fillings are in these chocolate candies, you can be sure that sugar is a large part of every one. Chocolate by itself is somewhat bitter.

most familiar sugar is *sucrose*. This is sometimes called *table sugar* because it is commonly found on dining tables.

Table sugar comes from two main sources: sugarcane and sugar beets (see p. 22). After refining, the resulting sugar is the same, no matter which its source.

Sugar was first refined by people in India well over 2,000 years ago. They gave us our name for sugar, which they called *sarkara*. However, for most of history the main sweetener was honey (see p. 15), which is made of different forms of sugar. Another traditional sweetener in North America is maple syrup (see p. 19). In the last few decades corn syrup has also become a popular sweetener (see p. 8).

Sugars are almost pure energy, supplying our bodies with the fuel needed to keep on living (see p. 10). Indeed, refined sugars are the purest foods of all, since they contain almost nothing but energy-providing substances.

However, we cannot rely on sugars alone, for they provide none of the other nourishing things our bodies need. In addition, sugars can cause cavities in our teeth, and some people's bodies have problems processing sugar (see p. 13). Chemists have developed some artificial sweeteners that do not cause such problems, though some such substitutes have caused other problems, such as increasing the risk of cancer.

Cotton candy is sugar spun into thin threads and twirled on a stick, a classic at fairs and carnivals. Because it is pure sugar, it is pure delight to many.

What Is Sugar?

Sugar is not just one substance but rather a whole range of them. Sugars all taste sweet and dissolve readily in water, making them enormously useful as sweeteners in all kinds of foods and drinks.

Sugars are all *carbohydrates*, which simply means that they are made of the elements (basic substances) carbon, hydrogen, and oxygen. Carbon, hydrogen, and oxygen can combine to make many, many different compounds (mixed substances). These compounds only differ in the number and arrangement of the elements.

Sugars are the simplest group of carbohydrates, formed of carbon plus water (which is made of hydrogen and oxygen). That's the source of the name *carbohydrate*, which means "watered carbon."

Where Sugar Comes From

Plants make sugar. In the process they keep themselves—and also the animals of the world—alive. In general, it works this way:

As plants grow, their green leaves use sunlight, carbon dioxide (a common gas) from the air, and water

Some people have problems digesting lactose, a sugar in milk and other dairy products. Today, however, they can take special pills that help break down the milk so they can get nourishment from it without becoming ill.

(drawn in through roots in the ground) to make various sugars in a process called *photosynthesis*. These sugars are the plant's main energy source. Humans and other animals eat parts of the plants for food, getting from them sugar for energy plus other nutrients (nourishing substances).

Only a few plants contain enough sugars to make them suitable for cultivation—that is, for deliberately growing or tapping for their sugars. The two main plants cultivated for sugar are the sugarcane and the sugar beet (see p. 22). Other traditional plant sources include some maple and palm trees (see p. 19), while corn has become a modern source of liquid sweetener. Honeybees use sugars from plants to make the oldest natural sweetener: honey (see p. 15).

Main Kinds of Sugars

One of the main kinds of sugar is *glucose* (from a Greek word for "sweet"). Glucose (also called *dextrose*) is commonly found in fruits and honey. It is also the main kind of

Plants use sunlight to create many kinds of sugars, which they store in stems and fruits. These apples, for example, are about 6 percent fructose (fruit sugar), 4 percent sucrose, and 1 percent glucose.

energy-providing sugar found in the blood of humans and other animals. It is also part of liquid nourishment given to medical patients *intravenously* (dripped directly into a vein).

Both plants and animals store extra glucose for future use. Plants store it in the form of *starch*. Each unit of starch is composed of thousands of units of glucose. Humans and other animals store excess glucose as *glycogen*. This is converted back to glucose when needed.

Another main kind of sugar is *fructose* (*fruit sugar*), found in fruits, honey, syrups, and some vegetables. The sweetest of all the natural sugars, fructose is sometimes used as a preservative to prevent food from spoiling.

A widely used modern sweetener is *high fructose corn syrup* (HFCS). This is made by breaking down the starch stored as energy reserves in corn. Corn syrup is cheaper than the other main sources of sugar and remains liquid when heated, so it is widely used for sweetening many foods, such as sodas and baked goods.

The most familiar natural sugar is the table sugar sucrose. In liquid form sucrose is a key sweetener used in many kinds of foods and drinks. In pure "refined" form (see p. 27), sucrose exists as *crystals*. These are solid forms with flat, regularly repeating sides, like the crystals found in a sugar bowl on a dining table.

Sucrose is actually formed of one

Below are highly magnified crystals of sucrose, like those from a package of common table sugar (left). These crystals could come from either the sugarcane or sugar beet, for the refined crystals are the same, no matter which the source.

unit of glucose linked to one unit of fructose (minus some water). Because it contains two units of sugar, sucrose is called a *disaccharide* (double sugar). Glucose and fructose are simple one-unit sugars, so they are called *monosaccharides*. Most other carbohydrates, such as starch, are composed of many, many sugar units. These are called *polysaccharides*.

Two other common sugars are also disaccharides. One is *maltose*, also called *malt sugar*, which is formed by the body as it breaks down starch. Maltose is formed of two glucose units joined together.

The other is *lactose*, also called *milk sugar* because it is found in milk. Lactose is made of two sugars: glucose and *galactose*. Some people's bodies have trouble digesting—that is, breaking apart—lactose, so eating milk products makes them feel ill.

Glucose powers all of our activities, day and night. As this man is jumping rope, his body is getting energy by using glucose from a recent meal or drawing on glycogen reserves in his liver and muscles.

Energy for Life

Like gasoline in an automobile, the sugar *glucose* is the fuel that powers our bodies. It provides the energy to keep our hearts beating and our lungs breathing—even when we're asleep.

Simple one- or two-unit sugars such as glucose, fructose, and sucrose (see p. 7) are easy for our bodies to digest—that is, to break down for energy use. Because of that, they give us a quick "rush" of energy. That's one reason why sugars are so attractive.

The problem is that a flood of sugar-based energy can overtax our bodies. Simple sugars are *refined* (see p. 27), so the body has to do little work to get at the energy in them. However, our bodies are more geared to handle sugars in their natural (unrefined) form. Because it takes longer for our bodies to break down unrefined sugars,

Fruits and vegetables like these contain a lot of natural sugar, but they do not create a "sugar rush." That is because they also contain a lot of other plant matter that the body breaks down more slowly, so the sugars do not go into the body all at once.

the sugar-based energy goes into our bodies more slowly and evenly, rather than in a flood. That is one reason why eating fresh fruit—even when it contains a lot of sugar—is much healthier than eating candy. (Another is that fruit contains many other nutrients.)

Especially in the richest countries of the world, many people eat far more food than their bodies need. The excess sugar is converted into glycogen (see p. 8) and stored mostly in the liver and the muscles.

When the body needs more energy, it taps the glycogen. This is then broken down again into easy-to-use glucose.

Sugar Balance

The body has a complicated set of mechanisms to keep the right amount of glucose available when it is needed. At different times during the 24-hour day, the body releases certain chemicals called *hormones*. Some of these control the balance of glucose in the blood.

Breakfast gives your body much-needed nourishment plus energy in the form of glucose to start the day. The orange juice, for example, is a good form of quick glucose energy.

When you wake up in the morning, you normally have not eaten for some hours. However, hormones trigger the body to raise the level of glucose in the blood in preparation for the new day. The body does this by tapping its glycogen reserves and converting some into quick-energy glucose.

When you eat breakfast, your body begins digesting the food, in the process releasing glucose to start powering you through the day. The same thing happens with the other meals of the day.

Often your meal gives you more glucose than you need at the moment. Then some glucose is removed from your bloodstream and stored in liver and muscle cells. On the other hand, if your body runs short of energy in between meals, hormones will again trigger the release of some energy reserves.

Finally at night, as you prepare to go to sleep, the body "powers down," like a computer going to "sleep." Then the blood has low levels of glucose again until the early morning.

Sugar Problems

Sometimes this complicated glucose-management system does not work properly. That can happen in the short term if you are sick or under extreme stress. However, people with a condition called *diabetes* have long-term problems with handling sugar.

The problem centers on *insulin*. This key hormone helps the cells that make up our bodies take in glucose and use its energy. However, some people's bodies either do not produce enough insulin to handle the amount of glucose in the bloodstream or cannot use the insulin properly to move glucose into the cells.

Then sugar builds up in the bloodstream, a condition called *hyperglycemia*. The body's kidneys try to flush out the excess sugar in urine, so the body calls for more water. In fact, one of the most notable early symptoms of diabetes is constant thirst. If the condition is untreated, the body's blood-delivery system (the *cardiovascular system*), including the heart, can be damaged, along with other parts of the body.

Meanwhile the cells that keep the body running are being starved for fuel. Since the cells are not receiving glucose, the body starts to burn fat as an alternative source of energy. However, this releases sub-

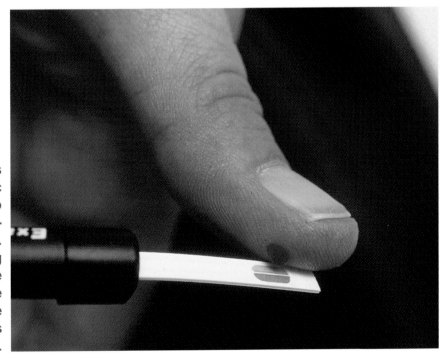

People with diabetes can use an electronic monitoring device to find out how much glucose is in their blood. They do this by placing a drop of blood on the end of a disposable strip inserted into the device, which produces a glucose reading.

stances called *ketones* into the blood. As they build up in the blood, ketones throw the body's chemistry out of balance. Over time the person will become ill, may fall into a coma (a state of deep unconsciousness), and may even die. In fact, before the 1920s most people with serious diabetes died of the condition, then sometimes called the *sugar disease*.

Then in the 1920s doctors discovered insulin and learned that insulin injections could help control severe diabetes. Today people with diabetes can live full, long, and active lives. They use small electronic devices to help them monitor the level of glucose in their blood. When necessary, they can give themselves in-

jections of the appropriate amount of insulin.

Many people have less serious forms of diabetes. These can often be treated by controlling sugar intake and by losing weight and exercising, which help the body use glucose better.

Some people also have problems converting excess glucose into glycogen. Their condition is known as *glycogen storage disease*. Some forms of this rare condition are treated by a special diet, but other forms can be fatal.

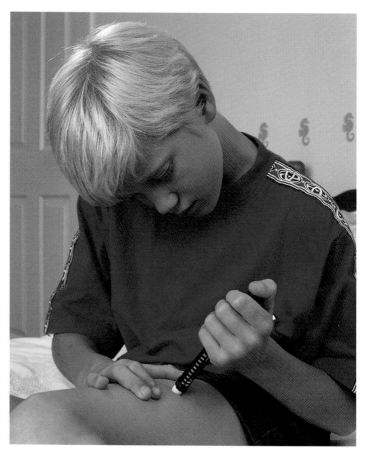

This young boy is giving himself an injection of insulin to help his body use glucose better. Instead of the usual type of needle, he is using a penlike device to inject the medicine.

Honey is often collected, purified, and bottled for sale, as in the jar at the top, but sometimes it is left in sections from the honeycomb, like that on the plate below.

The Taste of Honey

Probably the oldest source of concentrated sugar is honey. This comes from plants by way of honeybees.

Many flowering plants produce a sweet, syrupy liquid called *nectar*. This watery solution contains fructose, glucose, and sucrose (see p. 7). Various insects, as well as hummingbirds and fruit-eating bats, are drawn to the nectar. (Sweet drinks are always attractive. In Greek and Roman mythology, nectar was a drink of the gods.)

However, honeybees suck up nectar from the flowers and convert it into honey. They often seek out plants with nectar that has a high concentration of sugars. (Nectars

Honeybees visit flowers to suck up their sweet nectar, as this honeybee is doing on a daisy. In the process they also collect and scatter some of the dustlike pollen produced by the flower.

can contain as little as 3 percent to as much as 80 percent sugars.) Nectar also contains small amounts of other substances, so the resulting honey often carries the flavor of the plants' nectar. Clover honey, made from the nectar of the clover plant, is especially prized. Depending on the source, the color of honey can also vary, generally ranging between yellow and brown.

As the bees convert nectar into honey, much of the sucrose is changed into fructose and glucose, and much of the water is removed.

(Honey is only about 16 to 18 percent water.) The bees store the resulting very sweet liquid in *honeycombs*. These are networks of compartments made of beeswax, also produced by the honeybees.

Honeybees live together in large colonies in structures called *hives*, which are built around and protect honeycombs. In nature bees might build a hive in a hollow or notch in a tree, but they also live in hives built by humans. In earlier times humans often built conelike hives, sometimes made of straw.

Today beekeepers usually build hives shaped like boxes, which can be easily transported. This is important because many farmers and gardeners rely on bees. As they suck the nectar, bees spread *pollen*, a dustlike material produced in flowers, to other flowers. Many flowering plants need dustings of this pollen in order to grow properly and produce fruit.

Wild honeybees build hives in holes and cracks in places like trees and rocks. This is a natural hive in a tree in Ontario, Canada. Humans and other beings, such as bears, have long raided such hives for their honey.

Pollination is so important that beekeeping is a big business. Bees and their beehives are sent by truck hundreds of miles, following the spring from farm to farm as the blossoms open, to pollinate apple trees, cucumber plants, almond trees, and many other crops.

Bees are not domesticated (tamed). They are still wild, and their stings can be painful and dangerous. However, over many centuries humans have learned how to work with bees. Beekeepers wear protective clothing to avoid stings. They also use smoke to calm the bees, making them less likely to sting.

Drawings that date back thousands of years show people gathering honey from beehives. Today humans still gather honey from beehives, but the process has in some regions become a large-scale operation.

Traditionally people took sections of the honeycomb and let the thick, sweet liquid drip out into a container. Today this process is improved by the use of *centrifuges*. These are machines with spinning drums that create *centrifugal force*, the force that causes you to lean toward the outside on a whirling merry-go-round. This forces the honey out of the honeycomb, so it can be collected.

The honey is then heated to kill organisms that might cause illness and strained to remove unwanted particles, such as pieces of beeswax

(Left) Honeybees convert nectar from flowers into honey, filling the many cells in the honeycombs in their beehives.

Modern beekeepers keep their bees in boxlike hives, so they can easily be stacked and trucked from place to place. These beekeepers are checking a section of honeycomb pulled from a hive. They have calmed the bees with smoke, but still wear protective gear over their heads and necks.

and grains of pollen. Finally it is bottled for sale. Sometimes, however, honey is left in the comb, which is cut up, packaged, and sold in sections.

Honey is initially liquid. However, if it is allowed to sit for a time, some of it gradually turns into crystals or granules (grainlike particles) of sugar. When liquid and granulated honey are blended together, the result is a smooth, spreadable mixture called *creamed honey*. Whatever the form, honey is produced all over the world, wherever there are flowering plants and honeybees.

Maple syrup is a favorite topping for pancakes and waffles, as here.

Maple Syrup and More

Trees (and other plants) are nourished by *sap*, a fluid that circulates water and nutrients. Some tree saps are sweet enough to attract human interest.

The best-known source of sugar-rich sap is the sugar maple (known to biologists as *Acer saccharum*). Native Americans learned how to tap maples for their sap. They could do this only early in the springtime, when the weather veers between freezing and thawing. If a hole is drilled into the side of the tree in this period, sap will flow out and can be collected.

The sap is not very sweet, being about 97 to 98 percent water, but it is boiled in open pans to remove water, a process called *evaporation*. (Early Native Americans sometimes froze sap and then removed the ice, which was mostly water, leaving unfrozen maple syrup behind.)

Late winter is what people in northeastern North America call *sugaring time*. That's when they collect sap from the sugar maple, often in buckets like these, and convert it into tasty maple syrup.

Either way, to get just one gallon of maple syrup, you must start with about 30 to 50 gallons of sap!

Native Americans taught early European colonists how to make maple syrup. The methods they used remained much the same for centuries.

However, modern technology brought changes in the late 20th century. In place of buckets hanging from a taphole, many farmers began to use plastic bags or sometimes plastic tubing leading to a central collection tank. Instead of small family or community saphouses, where the syrup was boiled down, large factories were built to handle the evaporation, bottling, and packaging of the syrup. Syrupmakers also developed safer, more sanitary ways of creating syrup.

Maple syrup is still produced only in North America, home of the sugar maple. The main areas of commercial production are Quebec and Ontario in Canada and Vermont, New York, Wisconsin, Ohio, Michigan, New Hampshire, Pennsylvania, Massachusetts, and Maine in the United States.

Palm Sap

Elsewhere in the world other kinds of trees, primarily palm trees, are tapped for their sugary sap. This is often boiled down into a sticky brown sugary paste.

However, sometimes palm sap is allowed to "spoil" in a controlled way, in a series of chemical changes

This man in Burma is making an unrefined brown sugar called *jaggery* from the sap of a palm tree, using methods centuries old.

called *fermentation*. During this process the sugars in the sap are converted into carbon dioxide gas plus an alcoholic drink called *palm wine* or *toddy*. (In some regions the sap itself is also called *toddy*.)

The palm wine may have even more water driven off in a process called *distillation*. This produces a more highly alcoholic drink called *arrack*.

Palm trees grow best where the climate is warm, and palm sugar is generally produced locally on a small scale. However, palm sap is more easily converted into sugar than maple sap, for it contains less water and more sugar.

The main sources of palm sugar are the wild date palm, grown widely in India; the sugar (*Gomuti*) palm, grown widely in Southeast Asia, including the Philippines; the palmyra (*Borassus*) palm, grown in dryer regions of southwestern Asia; and the nipa palm, grown in watery regions of Southeast Asia. Palm sugar production is most widespread in Burma, India, and Cambodia.

Sugarcane (*Saccharum officinarum*) is believed to have originally come from the island of New Guinea in the southwestern Pacific Ocean. At left is a modern stand of sugarcane growing near Port Moresby, New Guinea. Above is a close-up view of the tough sugarcane stems, with buds forming between the sections.

Sugarcane, Sugar Beets

The main source of sugar has for centuries been the sugarcane (*Saccharum officinarum*), a member of the very large grass family. Unlike lawn grass, sugarcane grows very tall—often 18 feet or more—and has a heavy, tough stem. This stem contains the sugary sap that nourishes the cane. From early times people would chew on the sugarcane for its sweet juices.

Sugarcane was probably first grown as a crop on the Pacific island of New Guinea. Sugarcane farming spread from there to other nearby islands, perhaps starting about 8000 B.C. Sugarcane cultivation probably reached India by about 6000 B.C., spreading later to China and elsewhere in southeastern Asia and the Pacific, including Hawaii.

By about 500 B.C. people in India

had begun to learn how to refine sugar (see p. 27). Europeans probably first met sugarcane and the refined sugar made from it in India, when Greeks under Alexander the Great arrived there in the 300s B.C.

Sugarcane reached Persia (now Iran) much later, probably by about 600 A.D. From there sugarcane cultivation spread quickly to other parts of southwestern Asia and to Africa and Mediterranean Europe, especially Spain and southern Italy. However, most parts of Europe are too cool and dry for sugarcane to grow, so sugar was grown elsewhere and imported to Europe. Sugarcane did not reach the Americas until the 1490s, when Christopher Columbus brought it to the Caribbean.

Until that time refined sugar had been a rare luxury in Europe, available only in small amounts to rich people. However, sugar became a big business in the Americas, and sugar came to be available in larger amounts and to many more people.

To feed Europe's hunger for sugar, slaves were forced to do the hard and heavy work of growing and cutting the cane and extracting (drawing out) the sugar from it. The pattern of slavery in the Americas was, from the start, closely tied to sugar cultivation.

The work was so hard—and new slaves were so cheap to import—that slaves were often worked in the sugarcane fields until they died.

The sugarcane is a kind of tall grass that can grow to 18 feet high. At one stage in its life it puts out beautiful tassels, like those on the cane in this Florida field.

23

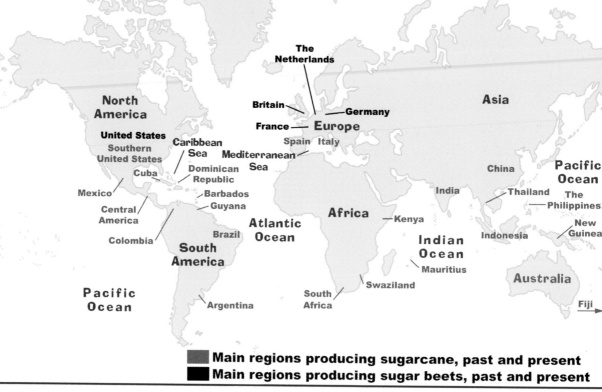

Arctic Ocean

The Netherlands

North America

Britain — Germany

France — Europe

Asia

United States

Spain Italy

Caribbean Sea

Mediterranean Sea

Pacific Ocean

Southern United States

Cuba

Dominican Republic

China

India

Thailand

The Philippines

Mexico

Barbados

Guyana

Africa

Kenya

New Guinea

Central America

Atlantic Ocean

Indonesia

Colombia

Brazil

South America

Indian Ocean

Mauritius

Australia

Pacific Ocean

South Africa

Swaziland

Argentina

Fiji

Main regions producing sugarcane, past and present
Main regions producing sugar beets, past and present

That would be true until slavery was gradually abolished in the Americas during the 1800s. However, the pattern of using slaves—and later poorly paid, overworked laborers, sometimes imported for the purpose—to produce sugar would be followed in most colonies and countries around the world.

Sugarcane is primarily a crop of the world's hot, humid regions. In the Americas the prime sugar-producing regions include the Caribbean islands (especially Barbados, Cuba, and the Dominican Republic),

Brazil, Central America, Mexico, Argentina, Guyana, Colombia, and the southern United States. In Asia and Oceania the main sugarcane producers are India, Indonesia, the Philippines, Thailand, Australia, and the island nation of Fiji. In Africa they are Swaziland, Kenya, South Africa, and the island of Mauritius.

Growing and Harvesting Sugarcane

Sugarcane is a *perennial* plant, meaning that it lives and grows for at least several years. Stalks of unripe cane are planted in the ground and covered lightly with soil, usually in fall or spring. This can be done by hand or machine.

The plant takes about 12 to 16 months to reach maturity. Then the sugarcane is harvested by cutting. This hard, difficult work was traditionally done by hand, using heavy knives such as *machetes*. Most sugarcane continues to be cut by hand, though increasing amounts have been harvested by machine since the 1940s.

Sugarcane fields are often burned before harvesting. This burns off the leaves that can dull knife blades and drives out unwanted creatures, such as rats and snakes, without harming the cane. Such burning damages the environment, however, so it is no longer done in some places.

After harvesting, sugarcane plants begin to grow again. They will normally be harvested eight to ten times, before the plants begin to weaken and fresh plants are started. In some warm countries, such as

(Left) After the leaves have been burned off, workers move in to cut down the sugarcane, as here in the Caribbean island of Martinique. They use sharp, heavy knives, but even so the work is very hard. (Below) Today sugarcane is often harvested by machines, which cut the plants off at ground level and load them into dump trailers, as in this field in Florida. The sugarcane is then shipped to a sugar mill for processing and refining.

Much of the sugar around the world today, especially in Europe, comes from the sugar beet plant. These are mature sugar beets growing in Britain. The soil has been moved aside to uncover the root, which is normally underground.

Cuba, the Philippines, and Colombia, crops may grow and be harvested throughout the year. In other countries harvesting is seasonal.

Sugar Beets

The other main modern source of sugar is the sugar beet (*Beta vulgaris*). The sugar is concentrated in the beet's white-fleshed underground root.

Sugar beets grow from seeds, which are sown early in the spring. Before being harvested in late autumn, the root grows to about one to two kilograms (2.2 to 4.4 pounds). During harvesting, the leafy tops are cut off (and sometimes used as animal feed) and then the beets are dug up, generally by machines.

The sugar beet has been grown for food in many parts of Europe and Asia since at least the first century A.D. Sugar was first extracted from beets in Germany in the 1740s. However, sugar beets did not become commercially important until the early 1800s, when the French were cut off from Caribbean sugar by blockades during the Napoleonic Wars. By the late 1800s beet sugar had overtaken sugarcane as the main European source of sugar, though sugarcane continued to lead elsewhere in the world.

Sugar beets grow best in temperate climates, especially in Europe and North America. The most important producers are France, Germany, Britain, the Netherlands, and the United States.

To get the sugary juices out of the sugarcane, the tough stem is crushed, pressed, and squeezed. Today that is done by machine, but for many centuries humans often provided the needed muscle power, as here.

Making Sugar

The traditional way to extract sugar from cane was to crush and squeeze the cane so the juice flowed out. Humans or animals, and later wind and sometimes water, were used to power the crushing devices. The juices were then boiled down to a brownish sugary paste that was mostly used locally, because it did not last long.

By around 500 B.C. people in India learned how to refine sugar so that it would last longer and could be transported. They put the brown paste in a cone-shaped container with a hole at the bottom and kept draining water through it. The water took out most of the impurities, leaving a cone-shaped "loaf" of white crystals. (That is why a pointed

This man in India is making a brown unrefined sugar paste. In some areas it is still used as is, but people in India discovered centuries ago how to refine it. In most industrial countries today this sugar paste would be refined into the familiar white sugar crystals.

mountain was traditionally nick-named "sugarloaf.") Up into the early 1900s sugar was still often sold in the form of a pointed sugar-loaf. People would cut off a chunk of sugar when they needed it. Until sugarcane began to be heavily culti-vated in the Americas (see p. 23), however, refined sugar was rare and expensive.

Extracting Sugar

Sugarcane must be processed within 24 hours of harvesting, so factories for extraction are placed near the cane fields. Cut into small pieces and often shredded, the cane is sent through a series of heavy rollers (*mills*), where it is further crushed and washed to extract more sugar. Alternatively the shredded cane can be soaked in special tanks to draw off the sugar. The leftover cane (*bagasse*) is often used as a fuel.

The sugary juice is then boiled with lime and filtered to remove impurities. The resulting clear, con-centrated syrup is boiled again and again to remove much of the water. As it becomes more concentrated, brownish crystals called *raw sugar* form within a thick syrup called *molasses*. The mixture is put into a spinning drum called a *centrifuge* (see p. 27). This separates the crys-tals from the thick molasses syrup and dries the crystals.

Molasses still contains a good deal of sugar, but this cannot be extracted economically. Instead molasses is used for a variety of purposes, such as for animal feed and for making various kinds of alcohols, including a drink called *rum* and a fuel to run automobiles.

Almost two-thirds of the raw sugar is either used as is or is bleached white to produce *plantation white sugar (mill sugar)*. The rest is sent for further refining, often to distant factories nearer where the sugar will be sold and used.

After being washed and sliced, sugar beets are soaked for their sugary juices and then are treated simi-

larly. However, unlike sugarcane, they can be stored safely, so extraction and refining are often done at the same factory.

Modern Refining

At the refineries sugar crystals are washed and remelted. Then more impurities are removed, which causes the color to turn to white.

Some sugar is left in less refined form as *brown sugar*. The rest is 99.8 percent pure white sucrose. Brown or white, the sugar crystals are then dried, packaged (in either crystal, cube, or powder form), and shipped or stored for sale and future use.

At sugar refineries the concentrated syrup containing molasses and crystals of raw sugar is put into a centrifuge like these. As it spins at high speed, the machine separates out the sugar crystals from the liquid molasses.

Words to Know

Acer saccharum: See MAPLE SYRUP.

bagasse The remains of the SUGARCANE stem after the sugary juices have been extracted.

Beta vulgaris: See SUGAR BEET.

carbohydrates Substances made of carbon, hydrogen, and oxygen. Found in the cells of every living thing, carbohydrates are necessary to human life. Sugars are all carbohydrates.

centrifuge A machine with a spinning drum that separates RAW SUGAR CRYSTALS from thick syrup (*molasses*) as juices from SUGARCANE or the SUGAR BEET are being extracted and concentrated.

crystal A solid form with flat, regularly repeating sides, as in common *table sugar* (see SUCROSE).

dextrose: See GLUCOSE.

diabetes A disease in which the body does not produce enough INSULIN or cannot use it properly, so it cannot get enough energy from GLUCOSE.

disaccharide A form of CARBOHYDRATE that contains two units of sugar, such as SUCROSE.

fructose (fruit sugar) The sweetest of the natural sugars, found in fruits, honey, syrups, and some vegetables; a simple one-unit sugar (MONOSACCHARIDE).

fruit sugar: See FRUCTOSE.

galactose: See LACTOSE.

glucose (dextrose) A simple one-unit sugar (MONOSACCHARIDE), commonly found in fruits and honey, a prime source of energy for many living things. Excess glucose is stored as GLYCOGEN in animals and STARCH in plants. People with DIABETES have trouble using glucose.

glycogen A CARBOHYDRATE that is the main form of energy storage for animals, which convert extra GLUCOSE into glycogen.

honey The oldest commonly used concentrated sweetener, formed by honeybees from the NECTAR of flowers.

hyperglycemia A damaging medical condition of too much GLUCOSE in the blood, as can happen with DIABETES.

insulin A chemical (*hormone*) released by the body to control the level of GLUCOSE in the blood and help the body use it for energy.

lactose (milk sugar) A kind of sugar formed of GLUCOSE and *galactose*; a DISACCHARIDE.

machete A heavy knife used in cutting SUGARCANE.

malt sugar: See MALTOSE.

maltose (malt sugar) A kind of sugar formed as the body breaks down STARCH. A DISACCHARIDE, it is formed of two units of GLUCOSE.

maple syrup A sweetener made of concentrated sap from the sugar maple tree (*Acer saccharum*).

milk sugar: See LACTOSE.

molasses: See RAW SUGAR.

monosaccharide A form of CARBOHYDRATE that contains one unit of sugar, such as GLUCOSE and FRUCTOSE.

nectar A sweet, syrupy liquid produced by flowering plants, containing FRUCTOSE, GLUCOSE, and SUCROSE. Honeybees collect the nectar and convert it into HONEY.

perennial A kind of plant that lives and grows for at least several years, such as SUGARCANE.

photosynthesis The process by which plants use sunlight, carbon dioxide, and water to make CARBOHYDRATES, including sugars.

polysaccharide A form of CARBOHYDRATE made of many units of sugar, such as STARCH.

raw sugar Brownish CRYSTALS that form within a thick syrup called *molasses* as juice from the SUGARCANE or SUGAR BEET is being concentrated.

refined sugar SUCROSE from which almost all impurities have been removed, turning brownish CRYSTALS (see RAW SUGAR) into white ones.

rum An alcoholic drink made from molasses (see RAW SUGAR).

Saccharum offinarum: See SUGARCANE.

starch A kind of CARBOHYDRATE, the main form of energy storage in plants. Each unit of starch is made of thousands of units of GLUCOSE.

sucrose (table sugar) The most familiar sugar, generally used in the form of white CRYSTALS, cubes, or fine powder (see REFINED SUGAR) made from the juices of the SUGARCANE or SUGAR BEET. A DISACCHARIDE, sucrose is formed of GLUCOSE plus FRUCTOSE, minus some water.

sugar beet (*Beta vulgaris*) A member of the beet family. Sweet juices from its white-fleshed root are a key source of SUCROSE.

sugarcane (*Saccharum officinarum*) A tall plant in the grass family. Sweet juices from its tough stem are the main source of SUCROSE.

table sugar: See SUCROSE.

On the Internet

The Internet has many interesting sites about sugar. The site addresses often change, so the best way to find current addresses is to go to a search site, such as www.yahoo.com. Type in a word or phrase, such as "sugar."

As this book was being written, websites about sugar included:

http://www.sugar.org/
Sugar Association website, offering facts, recipes, health information, and more.

http://www.sugaralliance.org/home.htm
American Sugar Alliance, an organization of people and companies that grow and process sugarcane, sugar beets, and corn, offering information and news.

http://www.nhb.org/
National Honey Board website, offering facts, recipes, research, links to other honey sites, and more.

http://maple.dnr.cornell.edu/produc/index.asp
Cornell Sugar Maple Research and Extension Program, offering facts about sap, trees, making syrup, recipes, and more.

In Print

Your local library system will have various books on sugar. The following is just a sampling of them.

Abbott, George C. *Sugar*. London and New York: Routledge, 1990.

Aykroyd, W. R. *The Story of Sugar*. Chicago: Quadrangle, 1967.

Galloway, J. H. *The Sugar Cane Industry: An Historical Geography from Its Origins to 1914*. New York: Cambridge University Press, 1989.

Haines, Gail Kay. *Sugar Is Sweet: And So Are Lots of Other Things*. New York: Atheneum, 1992.

Minitz, Sidney W. *Sweetness and Power: The Place of Sugar in Modern History*. New York: Viking, 1985.

Salunkhe, D. K., and B. B. Desai. *Postharvest Biotechnology of Sugar Crops*. Boca Raton, FL: CRC Press, 1988.

Van Nostrand's Scientific Encyclopedia, 8th ed., 2 vols. Douglas M. Considine and Glenn D. Considine, eds. New York: Van Nostrand Reinhold, 1995.

Vaughan, J. G., and C. A. Geissler. *The New Oxford Book of Plants*. New York: Oxford, 1997.

Index